Animals
That Live in Trees

by Jane R. McCauley

All day long, fruit bats rest upside down in trees.

BOOKS FOR YOUNG EXPLORERS
NATIONAL GEOGRAPHIC SOCIETY

Cuddly looking koalas live far away in Australia. There, they make their homes in tall eucalyptus trees. A koala and her baby nibble on the leaves, which give them food and water.

To climb, a koala digs its sharp claws into the bark. Safe and snug in the treetop, it sits and looks all around.

You can see a koala in the wild only in Australia.
But wherever trees grow, you will find many animals.
Trees give them safety, shelter, and food.

During the day, a screech owl rests in a tree hole.
A raccoon sometimes naps in a squirrel's empty nest.

Many kinds of birds nest in trees.
They find a lot of insects to eat.
Hungry baby woodpeckers open wide
for ants their parent brings. Young
vireos beg for the insect their mother
has caught. Baby birds eat and eat.

Insects are everywhere in the trees.
This cicada has squirmed out of its
"skin." A green katydid sits on a twig.

PILEATED WOODPECKERS

This hungry porcupine has stripped bark from a tree.
It eats bark, stems, leaves, and other parts of trees.
A porcupine can climb way up a tree, slowly but surely.
It may spend several days there. The animal could eat
so much bark that the tree would be damaged.

Monkeys called langurs live in Asia. Also called
leaf monkeys, they eat the leaves and fruit of trees.
These spotted deer like fruit, too. They find little bites
the langurs drop. One deer stretches to reach the leaves.

A howler monkey climbs way out on a limb to eat leaves.
How do you think this South American monkey got its
name? It howls and howls so other monkeys know it is there.

At night, a fruit bat flies away with a fig to eat.
Another goes after the fruit of a cashew tree. After
eating, the bats drop seeds that may grow into trees.

Thumbs on its wings help a little bat hold on
while it eats a big ripe fig. This bat has a body
about the size of a small mouse. Because they have
long snouts and pointed ears like foxes,
these bats are called flying foxes.

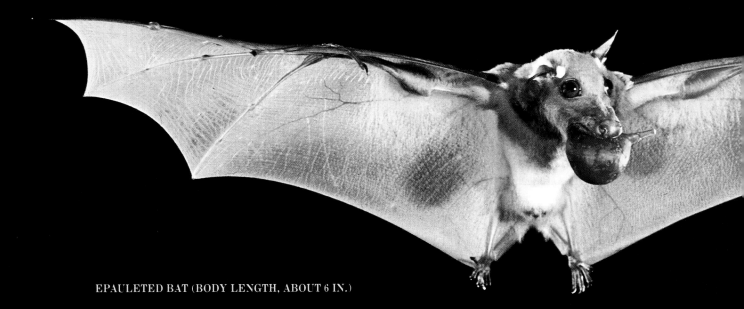

EPAULETED BAT (BODY LENGTH, ABOUT 6 IN.)

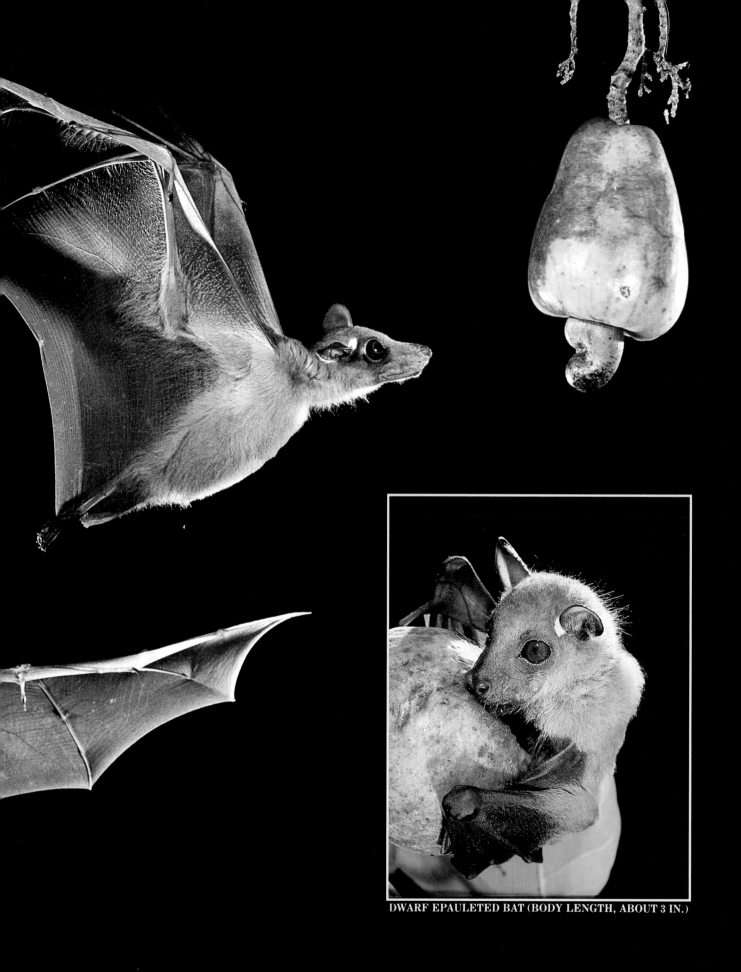

DWARF EPAULETED BAT (BODY LENGTH, ABOUT 3 IN.)

What do you think the pine marten sees? In the needles
of an evergreen branch, a little squirrel is hiding.
The pine marten is quick. It dashes through the treetops,
looking for a small creature. The squirrel is fast, too.
Maybe it will be lucky enough to get away!

These tree insects do not run and hide from danger.
Their shapes and colors help protect them.

A walkingstick sits very still and holds its front legs
straight out. It looks just like a twig. A treehopper
looks like the top thorn on a stem. On a pile
of leaves, a leaf insect almost disappears.

This animal with horns looks like a dinosaur, but it's a chameleon. Chameleons are lizards that change color and blend with their background. A tree frog matches the bark of a tree, and its enemies might not see it. But they may hear it sing, as its throat fills with air. This gecko, another kind of lizard, is almost impossible to see on the bark. Can you trace its shape?

JACKSON'S CHAMELEON

DISK-WING BAT

When you climb, how do you hold on?
These animals have special ways to hold on to
leaves and bark. As a snail glides up a tree,
it coats the bark with sticky slime.

Bats a little bigger than your thumb hang on
to a banana leaf with the suction cups
on their feet and wings. This gecko has rows of
tiny suction cups under its wide toes.

During the night, several creatures come to a eucalyptus tree to lick its sweet juice. How many can you count? All five animals are called gliders. Like koalas, gliders live mainly in forests in Australia.

A sugar glider has caught an insect to eat. This animal can glide from tree to tree, looking for food. Flying squirrels glide, too. Turn the page to find out how they do it.

A flying squirrel springs from a tree,
spreading its arms and legs. Its loose skin
stretches out like wings. The long, bushy tail
helps it steer. Young flying squirrels
playing outside their tree hole run and chase
each other up and down the trunk.

Just before sunset, a howler monkey
begins to move through the treetops
toward a resting place. It wraps its
strong tail firmly around a branch.
Then it reaches out with its hands
and goes from one tree to another.

The woolly monkey wraps its tail tightly around a branch. The strong tail helps the monkey keep its balance. It can also hang by its tail. A gibbon, a kind of ape, has no tail. It uses its long arms and fingers when it moves through the trees.

Using both its hands and feet, a young orangutan makes a nest of palm leaves. It bends the leaves with its fingers and holds them down with its feet. It builds a new nest to sleep in nearly every night.

The sloth makes its home high up in a rain forest, tucked away among the leaves. It spends a lot of time just hanging upside down by its long, curved claws. The sloth even eats this way. This animal can swim well, but on land it has a hard time getting around. It is built for living in trees.

Many creatures spend most of their lives in trees.
Night and day, all year long, they are moving about
on the branches, in the leaves, and even under the bark.

This sleepyhead, a koala nestled against a branch, may nap all day.

Cover: Is it safe to come out? A little saw-whet owl waits for dark before leaving its tree home.

Published by the National Geographic Society, Washington, D. C.
Gilbert M. Grosvenor, *President*
Melvin M. Payne, *Chairman of the Board*
Owen R. Anderson, *Executive Vice President*
Robert L. Breeden, *Senior Vice President, Publications and Educational Media*

Prepared by the Special Publications Division
Donald J. Crump, *Director*
Philip B. Silcott, *Associate Director*
Bonnie S. Lawrence, *Assistant Director*

Staff for this book
Jane H. Buxton, *Managing Editor*
John G. Agnone, *Picture Editor*
Pamela J. Castaldi, *Art Director*
Cinda Rose, *Consulting Art Director*
Peggy D. Winston, *Researcher*
Stuart E. Pfitzinger, *Illustrations Assistant*
Mary Frances Brennan, Vicki L. Broom, Carol R. Curtis, Mary Elizabeth Davis, Rosamund Garner,
    Virginia W. Hannasch, Artemis S. Lampathakis, Ann E. Newman, Cleo E. Petroff, Virginia A. Williams,
    Staff Assistants

Engraving, Printing, and Product Manufacture
Robert W. Messer, *Manager*
David V. Showers, *Production Manager*
George J. Zeller, Jr., *Production Project Manager*
Gregory Storer, *Senior Assistant Production Manager*
Mark R. Dunlevy, *Assistant Production Manager*
Timothy H. Ewing, *Production Assistant*

Consultants
Dr. Lynda Bush, *Reading Consultant*
Peter L. Munroe, *Educational Consultant*
Eirik A. T. Blom, Maryland Ornithological Society; Bela Demeter, Miles Roberts, Steven D. Thompson, National Zoological
    Park; Sally Love, Smithsonian Institution; Dr. Merlin D. Tuttle, Bat Conservation International, *Scientific Consultants*

Illustrations Credits

Art Wolfe (cover); Merlin D. Tuttle/Bat Conservation International (1, 12-13, 20 lower left); Jen and Des Bartlett (2-3, 32); Michael Fairchild/Peter Arnold, Inc. (4); VALAN/Albert Kuhnigk (5, 8-9); ANIMALS ANIMALS/Ted Levin (6); John F. O'Connor, M.D./PHOTO/NATS (7 upper); Breck P. Kent (7 middle, 17 lower left); Robert and Linda Mitchell (7 lower, 20-21); Gunter Ziesler/Peter Arnold, Inc. (10, 26-27); ANIMALS ANIMALS/Raymond A. Mendez (11); Wayne Lankinen (14-15); Clyde H. Smith/Peter Arnold, Inc. (16-17); ANIMALS ANIMALS/E. R. Degginger (17 lower right); ANIMALS ANIMALS/Zig Leszczynski (18-19, 19 right); John Gerlach/DRK PHOTO (19 upper left); Treat Davidson (20 upper); Rupert Russell/Australasian Nature Transparencies (22-23); Dave Watts/Australasian Nature Transparencies (23 right); ANIMALS ANIMALS/Mark Stouffer (24); ANIMALS ANIMALS/Richard Alan Wood (24-25); Vic Cox/Peter Arnold, Inc. (28 left); ANIMALS ANIMALS/Miriam Austerman (28 right); Rod Brindamour (28-29); Wolfgang Kaehler (30); Robert Lee II (31).

Library of Congress CIP Data
McCauley, Jane R., 1947-
    Animals that live in trees.
        (Books for young explorers)
        Summary: Introduces a variety of animals, such as koala, fruit bat, walkingstick, snail, and howler monkey, that
seek safety, food, and shelter in trees.
        1. Forest fauna—Juvenile literature. 2. Animals—Juvenile literature. 3. Trees—Juvenile literature. [1. Forest
animals. 2. Animals. 3. Trees] I. Title. II. Series.
    QL112.M34   1986   591.5'2642   86-12593
    ISBN 0-87044-636-3 (regular edition)
    ISBN 0-87044-641-X (library edition)

MORE ABOUT

Animals That Live in Trees

Though trees grow in many areas, we often do not realize the variety of animals that depend on them in one way or another. Many creatures make their homes there; others divide their time between the ground and the trees. They may climb trees in search of food, a place to rest, or to escape from predators.

Of all the animals in trees, insects are the most numerous. Yet we often overlook them because many are small and can hide easily under the bark, among the leaves, and even inside the wood. Some, such as tree-hoppers, leaf insects, and walking-sticks (16-17),* are camouflaged by colors and shapes that resemble different parts of plants.

On a walk in the woods in late summer, look closely up and down the bark of trees. You may find the "skins" of cicadas (7). When the cicadas emerge after spending years in the ground, they crawl up tree trunks and wiggle out of the hard outer skeletons that protected them as they grew. Pale, soft, and vulnerable for a few hours, they quickly turn darker and harden. On a hot day, listen for the loud chorus of cicadas. You may also be able to pick out the varied tunes of katydids (7).

Tree-living insects provide food for other tree residents such as birds (4, 6-7). Birds and their eggs, in turn, become meals for other animals such as martens (14-15). The parts of a tree—blossoms, seeds, shoots, bark, leaves, sap, fruits, nuts, and buds—nourish both residents and visitors.

Through their eating habits, fruit bats, called flying foxes (1, 12-13), help plant banana, fig, and other tropical trees. When they fly about at night, feeding on the fruits of the trees, bats drop large numbers of undigested seeds. They also pollinate certain tropical flowers that open in the evening. As they move from flower to flower, sipping nectar, bats spread the pollen.

Among tree dwellers, perhaps the fussiest eater is the koala (2-3, 32). This marsupial makes its home in eucalyptus trees in coastal forests and woodlands of Australia. More than 500 species of eucalyptus grow in Australia, but koalas consume the leaves of only about a dozen species. Koalas rarely drink, for they derive sufficient moisture from the leaves they eat.

Some animals are almost completely arboreal, spending virtually all their time in trees. The koala descends a tree mainly to walk to another one for more leaves. The sloth (30-31), which lives in the canopy of a rain forest, rarely goes to the ground more than once a week. Its long curved claws impede the sloth's progress on land. Like the koala, it is well adapted for life in the trees.

Scientists classify sloths as either two-toed or three-toed, depending on the number of toes on each front foot. Both kinds eat, sleep, mate, and give birth high up in the trees. Sloths hang motionless for hours; they are the slowest of all land mammals.

Another slow-moving animal is the tree snail (20). Making small, wave-like movements with its foot, it gradually works its way up a trunk. Sticky fluid secreted by glands in the snail's foot enables it to glide smoothly across rough bark.

VALAN / WAYNE LANKINEN

Special adaptations help some tree-dwelling animals find food. Overlapping tips of its bill enable a red crossbill to pry open the scales of a pinecone to get the seed.

Some of the more familiar ways animals get around in trees include leaping, flying, and swinging. A prehensile tail allows the woolly monkey (28) and the howler monkey (11, 26-27) to grip branches as they move through the canopy and the understory. The hairless tip of the tail is as sensitive as a human fingertip and is ridged like a fingertip.

Unlike most monkeys, gibbons (28) and other apes have no tails. Extremely long arms and fingers and flexible joints enable gibbons to maneuver easily in the trees. These lightweight apes swing by their arms from branch to branch, or brachiate, at amazing speed. They usually stay about 100 feet above the ground and are nimble enough to escape almost any predator.

*Numbers in parentheses refer to pages in *Animals That Live In Trees*.

Graceful as an acrobat, a gibbon travels through the trees by brachiating, or arm swinging. This multiple-exposure photograph shows how the agile ape brachiates on a rope. It pulls itself forward, hand over hand, with light, seemingly effortless movements. Using its long fingers as hooks, it swings by one arm, then the other. It lets go between handholds. When it travels along a limb, a gibbon usually walks upright, holding its arms up for balance.

Gibbons and orangutans (28-29), their relatives, live in the wild only in the rain forests of Southeast Asia. So it is unlikely that you can watch them unless you visit a zoo.

But wherever trees grow, they provide a chance for you and your child to discover a variety of animals, to see how they live, and to learn about the different ways they travel. You may need to visit a woods frequently, during different seasons and at different times of day. Why not begin your investigations with your child by trying some of these activities:

• Select a tree that you can visit each day for several weeks. Schedule your outings for the morning, afternoon, and early evening. Keep a record of any animals you find. Write down whether they have homes in the trees or just come and go. What do they eat? How do they hold on when they climb?

• In late summer take a walk in a woods. Remember that it is easy to scare animals into their hiding places. Be very still and listen carefully. Mosquitoes hum. Bees buzz.

Squirrels chatter. Can you hear the tap, tap of a woodpecker? Try to identify any other sounds you hear coming from the trees. Check the ground for any telltale tracks.

• For a rainy-day project, look back at the pine marten and squirrel on pages 14-15. Write a story telling what you think will happen to the squirrel. Will it get away?

• Plan a trip to a zoo to observe monkeys and apes. What differences can you see? Before your visit, gather some books from a library to help you identify the various kinds of monkeys and apes and learn where they live and how they move about.

• Draw a picture of a eucalyptus tree, a pine tree, and another tree you have seen. Then draw pictures of koalas or other animals in this book. Cut them out and place them in the kind of tree you think they inhabit.

With careful and repeated observations in natural settings, you can help your child discover the special world of trees and the ways many familiar animals depend on them for safety,

homes, and food. A visit to a zoo or an aquarium may provide your child the opportunity to learn about some of the more exotic arboreal animals: orangutans, sloths, gibbons, langurs, howler monkeys, koalas, geckos, and chameleons.

ADDITIONAL READING

Amazing Animals of Australia. (Washington, D.C., National Geographic Society, 1984). Ages 8-12.

Book of Mammals, 2 vols. (Washington, D.C., National Geographic Society, 1981). Ages 8 and up.

Creatures of the Woods, by T. Eugene. (Washington, D.C., National Geographic Society, 1985). Ages 4-8.

Koalas and Kangaroos: Strange Animals of Australia, by T. Eugene. (Washington, D.C., National Geographic Society, 1981). Ages 4-8.

The Primates, by S. Eimerl, I. DeVore, et al. (Alexandria, Va., Time-Life Books, 1980). Family reading.